MILLRAT

MILLRAT

poems by

Michael Casey

expanded edition

Adastra Press
Easthampton • Massachusetts
1999

ISBN 0-938566-81-4

Acknowledgments:
Harvard Magazine, New England Poetry Calendar, Schist, Aisling, The New Salt Creek Reader, Ethos and *the Slow Loris Press Broadside Series*.

Expanded Edition

First published by Adastra Press in 1996 as a limited edition chapbook.

This is a fictional work of poetry and the characters herein are not real people.

Adastra Press
16 Reservation Road
Easthampton, MA 01027

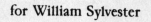
for William Sylvester

contents

driving while under
the influence

it was three AM and I hit
the blinking yellow light
on the route three rotary near Drum Hill
we got out quick
to throw away beer cans
and then I backed up the car a bit
and tried to go forward
but the car wouldn't go forward
so I backed up around the rotary
into a gas station
I figured I could put my car
in the row of cars already there
and nobody would notice   right?
I get out and hide behind but
by this time I can see the flashing lights
and it was really something
the police cruiser goes around the rotary
takes the exit I took
and comes right to me
I was alone   all my friends split
and they get me   for leaving the scene

driving under the influence
and being a minor in possession
all kinds of stuff   right?
I asked the guy found me
how'd you catch me?
he said he followed the leaking radiator
it leaked after the crash   right?
fifty million dumb cops in the world
and this guy
has to be a genius

the company pool

ya want ta be in our pool?
I was gonna axk ya sooner
but I didn't know
if ya wanted ta
I'll show ya how it works
ya pay a dollar an a quarter
ya givit ta me
but you'll haf ta start next week
the dollar goes inta the home run pool
and ya don't haf ta pay the quarter
unless if ya want ta
we use The Record
and we check out the runs column
on the sports page
not that this paper's always right
in fact it usually aint right
but this is the paper we use anyway
ya gotta use something ta go by
the team with the most runs
at the end a the week
the guy with that team wins the pool

the quarter is for the thirteen run pool
if ya team gets exactly thirteen runs
ya win that
that don't happen too often
Alfred over there
made thirty bucks last week winning that
so if ya want ta
ya can be in that one too
ya see we pick the team from this can
every week
so one guy don't get stuck
with the same shitty team
the tricky thing is
that the week for the pool
starts on Thursday and for the paper
it starts on Monday
so we just carry it over
y'understand this?

Sports News –
Softball Team

Eddie "Pop" Barnes, manager of the Lowell Textile Corporation Team, did not do too well for the first game of the season. The LTC team lost to the Farragut's Grill team 39 to 4. Said Eddie, "Their pitcher was just too much for our guys. You should have seen the arm she had." However, Edward, the ever hopeful, did promise that the team would do better in the future games. We sure hope they do.

Let's get out to Shedd Park's field and cheer for the LTC team for the Friday June 10th game at 7:00 PM with the team of the Hi Lite Cafe. Fan cheers can really do a lot to a team. We sure hope they do.

getting so

it's getting so
you can't drive a car
on the streets these days
without having some asshole
run inta ya car
denting it all over
or like
in my case
driving along the highway
and having
a guard rail jump out in front of the car
those fuckers are fast

coffee truck

the coffee truck once ran out
of Tahitian Treat at the mill
so for a long time I used to get Wink
and the coffee truck guy told me a story
he said the mending room girls
always used to get
Halfnhalf with their lunch
then for a long time
he couldn't get Halfnhalf
only Polynesian Punch
and when the guy got Halfnhalf back
they wouldn't touch it
they was so used
to getting Polynesian Punch
so when the guy got back Tahitian Treat
he thought I wasn't gonna touch it either
but I went right back
to getting Tahitian Treat
no more Wink for me after that
I fooled the guy
and he was surprised too

Walter's sore feet

I used to feel like
picking up my fuckin feet
putting em in my fuckin pocket
and walking on my fuckin knees
so now I do   what my chiropractor says
I spend ten minutes every night
rolling my feet each one
over a bunch of golfballs
in a shoe box
it's been helping me a lot
and once you get used to it
it's no trouble at all
since I started using two shoe boxes
it's cut the time in half

positivity poster

picture a grandmotherly lady on a rocker

> what's outdated about the textile
>   business
> we are
> not the new machinery we have
> or up to the minute end products
> but just our old fashioned ideas
>   avoiding waste
>   pride of craftsmen
>   work as a team
>   the worth of experience
> all these
> add to the unequaled quality
> at wholesale value
> that make our patrons love us
> the new old fashion
> textile business

everyone in the mill
the dye house anyway
reading this stuff would think

of only one word   bullshit
you can guess
what wall these posters were on
and without any effort at all
you memorize them
and with some creativity   and even art
you write crude phrases
and drawings on them
it was a lot like team effort
group improvement of a product

all I know

all I know is Hazel's
all shithouse at ya
she says
when Freddy Waite's
lookin for a good time
he only has one thing on his mind
and she don't want
her husband with ya
when ya lookin for it
that's all I know about it
that's all I'm gonna say

Maurice tells Roland to go somewheres play with his puppy

there goes ya brother
and I know you're French and
he's a Portygee
but he must be some kind of relation
or else
how come he's always calling you dad
could be y'know
all yis have to do's look at her
she gets pregnant
what's the number now?   eleven twelve?
maybe you lost track of this one
and a nice Portygee family
adopted him
maybe it wasn't their fault at all
that he turned out like you

Roland's trick

Roland knows this trick
you drive in a gas station
and say
fill it up ten dollars worth
and the guy fills it up all the way
say   fourteen fifteen dollars worth
and then Roland goes
I said just ten dollars
was all I wanted
and he only pays ten dollars
his advice is
you can't try this
twice with the same guy
but it works
with almost anybody
but for owners of the gas station
and don't   do not   try it
if the kid looks like a tardo
see this scar   goes Roland
a tire iron
when a tardo think he's being cheated
he don't have no self control

foreman

Walter walked over to Alfred
and asked him
to mix up the soap
when he got the chance
and Alfred said
sure   he'd do it
when he got the chance
but he never did it
so Walter walked over to Ronald
and said
Ron   why don't ya make the soap up
when ya through what ya doin
and Ronald said
fuck you Walter
of course
Ronald went and mixed up the soap
when he got the chance
Walter noticed it too
they didn't make Walter
the boss for nothing

positivity poster #75

perplexed??
be sure then to see your supervisor
PDQ   pretty darn quick

    picture of
    a man in a pickle
        in a rowboat with paddles
        floating away
        in a bowl of soup
        in a jar of jam
        in circles walking
        in a dog house

whether your trouble
is on the job or off
don't face it alone
have someone with you
on your side
your supervisor certainly
in every possible way
will help you

at the end of this I add
                OUT THE FUCKIN DOOR
I didn't disguise
my handwriting or anything
I knew Walter would blame Roland for it
as it turned
Walter liked the remark
and gave Roland all the credit

the night the fight with Bill happened

that same night
after they beat up Bill
they came back
don't you know
shithead was mad
because Ray broke up the fight
and so he brought back his gang
a bunch of them
clean out the mill
that's what he said
I'm gonna clean out the mill
the second shift upstairs
and the dye house
hears all the noise
and runs down and those
assholes left quick enough
through the doors
out the windows
only new guy got hurt

one of the dips
lost a shoe at the window
rushing out of it
sixteen year old kids
gonna beat up growd men
gonna clean out the mill?

cleaning out the mill

those two kids that beat up Bill
they came back on the weekend
and stole Jonesy's toolchest
the night watchman knew
they worked here and believed them
they say they have to repair
something at their house
you know which night watchman
Gilberto the Spanish kid
from Lowell Tech
and under his pitcher
at the company picnic
someone writes
did anybody see a toolchest
wicked funny
but Walter took it down
because he didn't
want to hurt
Gil's feelings
Walter a regular

barrel of laughs
you hear his story
about the golfballs?

mending room girl

there were some girls behind her too
gigglin   probably goosin each other
there was some girls
comin down the stairs
and one of them was swearin
swearin like a trooper
fuck this fuck that
and they turn the corner
and see Mo there
and Mo goes   hey
and the girl goes   oh
you know the girl
the one in orange
the blond with the boobies
like watermelons
the pretty one
with the tattoo
Mo won't swear
when a girl can hear
but what Mo should a said was
        hey watch ya fuckin mouth

but then she probably would a said
        hey mind ya own fuckin business
she probably would have

swivel hook

Mo was holdin the cloth
goin into the kettle
when a barbed needle
with a swivel hook on it
went through his hand
it was something
a mending room girl
forgot in the cloth
and he stopped the kettle rollers
somehow just in time
but it took a while
to get the needle out of the cloth
and then out of his hand
Mo swearin all the time
dumb fuckin cunt
yellin that towards the mending room
two hundred yards away
dumb fuckin cunt

break room

coffee break yesterday
one of the office girls
stops by the coke machine
and she is wearin a dress
and looks really fine
something like wrapped
in a pink towel with sparkling tights
and Mo is lookin at her
all the time she is there
and she's leavin
he goes
      hey you
and she turns around
and I am hiding my head in my arms
for what he's about to say
and he goes
      what a pretty dress

just one B & E

once they got me for sniffin glue
which almost don't count
cuz like it was nothin
and then there was just one B & E
was all they got me for
just one
but no more because I'm a good boy now
I promised my mother
but like if anybody
needs any power tools
lemme know by
before this weekend
cuz like as far's my mother's concerned
good boys are ones don't get caught

dye house

the same guy used to shine his shoes
with the cloth
that was goin into the kettle
while the kettle was heatin up
one day it looped round his foot
lifted him right up
his foot went through the eye
and got stuck in the rollers
with five hundred pounds pressure
the water wasn't hot
and his leg didn't go through the rollers
but still he hurt his foot
his arms his ribs his head
he was out of work for two months
how'd it happen?
gee
I don't know
must've stepped on it somehow
he gets back out of the hospital
and comes back to work

he's loadin kettle three
when Walter and me
come round the corner
we see him tryin the same thing again
shinin his shoes with the movin cloth
Walter says to him
out the fuckin door
and real quick
he was on the outside lookin in

Mill Security

from the Lowell Manufacturing Company
PRIDE
Personal Responsibility in Daily Effort

During the past several weeks there has
been several instances of sneaky theft in
the mill. Not only have company property
been taken but personal property as well.
Just last week our most serious trouble
involved several former and now sadly
accused, currently leaved without pay,
employees gaining entrance to the mill
illegally and assaulting the foreman on
duty. This we will not tolerate!! As an
immediate measure to protect employees
and property, a member of Lowell's
Police Department will be here on duty
in the mill from 5:00 P.M. until let out
in the morning.

Urgent Need for Blood

There is an urgent need in Massachusetts for blood donors. This seems to be an excellent opportunity for the company family to do something for the neighbors in our community. It's easy, painless, and really worthwhile.

> Here's How:
>> When: August 7th
>> Time: 12:00 to 2 PM Monday
>> Where: American Red Cross
>> 391 Lacoshua St., Lowell, Mass.
>> Blood types needed: ALL

The only prerequisite is that you must not have given blood within the last six weeks. Personnel wanting to donate blood may donate blood without loss of pay or attendance bonus provided you report back to work within ten minutes of consuming the five free cookies.

Transportation is free. Contact the personnel office now. Don't wait until the last minute! Due to an unfortunate accident after the last blood drive, personnel from the dye house are excluded from this offer.

same guy again

the same fuckin guy
before they had the caustic tank
they used to have flakes
and you had to mix the stuff
you had to be careful too
fuckin stuff would burn
this new guy
he throws a bucket of the stuff
into the kettle
it splashes back
his ass was on fire
runnin all over the dye house
Walter chasin after him
it was Fred and me caught him
and Walter helped us
throw him into the soap barrel
same fuckin guy
was gonna bring home
industrial peroxide
for his wife to dye her hair
Walter caught him then

just in time
of course right now
that guy is on the outside
lookin in

remember when

remember when
the overhead door slammed down
on that fat guy from Amalgamated Plastics
the guy was just standing there
and slap   out like a light
I wasn't there then
these guys here had to tell me about it
had to tell me about it later
it must have been funny as a bastard
though you actually seen it

maintenance

we don't got enough to do
maintenance can't lift barrels
we gotta lift the barrels
four hundred fifty pound barrels
I bring in a barrel
and then go back to maintenance
and there's
fuckin Roger back there doin nothin
fuckin John back there doin nothin
fuckin Willie back there doin nothin
Willie's eighty years old
I'm not axin him bring in no barrel
but what about fuckin Roger and John
you don't axk an eighty year old man
to bring in no fuckin barrel

Boisvert

I see the new guy
take the bar off the turntable and drop it
then he looks for Boisvert
Boisvert's the swing man
in the drier room
drop it again louder says Roland
and the new guy drops the bar again
with a louder noise
and Boisvert's movin trucks
near the dye house
looks up because he hears it
but he doesn't do anything
what happened was
yesterday Roland
told the new guy
to ask Boisvert
if Boisvert's girl was really a boy
Boisvert doesn't even talk to them now
doesn't bring them work
doesn't sew up the cloth
they think they hurt his feelings
but I know he's just lazy

when he was in the dye house
and we all take ten minute breaks
you know what he's do?
Boisvert takes fifteen minutes
we got rid of him
Boisvert just don't like to work
even if he's elsewheres in the mill
Walter doesn't like seein him around
Walter thinks Boisvert's the type
should be on the outside lookin in

positivity poster #76

picture of angry rhinoceros facing
hunter: the hunter is reaching for his rifle
but the gun bearer who looks like Oliver
Hardy with rifle is running away from the
hunter and toward a giant time clock

WHEN YOU LEAVE EARLY
SOMEONE ELSE
SUFFERS FOR IT
SOMEONE ELSE
HAS TO WORK HARDER
LET US BE FAIR
FROM NOW ON

the end of every day now
Roland runs to the time clock
yellin RHINO RHINO RHINO

vindication

I told Ronald
I like the German car
but the big drawback
was I didn't understand
the German on the radio
he believed me about that
and everybody laughed
at him when they found out
later when I was
knocked senseless
in the great mill invasion
it was Ronald got me out of it
it's pretty rough
when you're in so much hurt
a little shit
has to help you out of it

forklift driver

the forklift driver
fucked up the elevator again
he tried to drive the forklift in it
when the door was still closed
this is the third day in a row
somethin like that happened
I'd say to him
don't even bother ta punch out
just leave
it'd be worth the week's pay or so
just to get rid of him
do you know how important
that fuckin elevator is?
Lou is up there yellin all over for yarn
because he can't get it
and this is holdin up the knittin room
knappin room and the whole place
is gonna be backed up now
they tell me Lou
is pissin an moanin up there
like he was pissin razor blades

3230 polyester

Ronald is in the aisle
of the drier room
and can't find anywhere
to put the full truck
he is pushin he's lookin all around
and Omer from the dye house
sees this
yells out
RONALD
and Ron turns around
thinkin Omer's goin
to tell him where
to put the truck
of 3230 polyester
and Omer yells out
SHOVITUPYAFUCKINASS

desert boots

I was callin from the police station
at 4 AM
and I'm sayin to myself
let it be Dad answers the phone
let it be Dad don't let Ma answer
and so after thirty dial rings
my Mother answers the phone
I say real nice and quiet
Ma   could I speak to Dad please?
she must have known from my tone
I was not being wiseass
that something was wrong
she says OK and I tell my Father
what happens how I am at the station
for drunk drivin leavin the scene
bein a minor in possession
and how the car is all messed up
so please come and get me   Dad
I tell all this story
not even guessing
my Mother's on the extension
I get home and finally crash on the bed

with my clothes on
just takin off my desert boots
hangin them up on the floor
while I am sleepin
who goes out and checks out
the scene of my latest crash
but my Mom and Dad
they were impressed with the damage
and as soon as they return home
here I am in a deep sleep
and I slowly begin to notice
someone poundin in my face
with as pair of desert boots
I am yellin   Ma   Ma   helpme helpme
but I was all mixed up
it was my Ma hittin me
and my Father who stops her
it was my Dad actually saves me
those boots were really heavy
and really hurt
and I started acting careful after that
wearin sneakers from then on

Alfred Waite brings in the wrong cloth

Walter: Al   I told ya a thirty twenty for
four not a thirty twenty-four for
four

Ronald: you can't tell him nothin

Roland: too much of this
when he was little

Mo: watch it   Freddy
you'll be on the outside
lookin in

resignation

they don't like my work here
I'm quittin
a friend of mine
his uncle owns a gas station
I can get a job there
pumpin gas
whiles I'm lookin
for somethin better
hey Walter
catch this   I'll say
and I'll throw a hook at him
when he throws it back
I'll say
don't you throw nothin at me
fuck this place
I'm leavin

my youngest that tall

my youngest that tall
they kept on sendin him home last year
the fuckin kid was always actin up
so last summer
all through the summer
they were buildin a new school
near the house
and we kept on
pointin out the fuckin thing
tryin to get the kid interested you know
see the school they're buildin for you
that sure is a nice-lookin school
so my wife takes him
to the second grade to register
and the kid looks around him
and right in front of the teacher
he says to her
I aint stayin in this fuckin place
my wife said she felt about this fuckin tall

Mill News

DEPARTURES

Congratulations for Joe Bonmarche (knitting) on his retirement. Don't work too hard with the golf Joe!

Best wishes for Magloire "Muggy" Houle with his new job at Crane Knitting.

Best wishes for Gerard Boisvert (drier room) with his new job plans

Good luck for Ronald Beausoliel (dye house) in his criminal justice studies and his work at Dino's Oldsmobile and Shell Station.

CONGRATULATIONS

Congratulations for Florette Boisvert's (knitting) citation from the Captain of

the Queen Anna Maria for her rendition
of "La Vie en Rose."

TERMINATIONS

We hope that the two former employees
of maintenance and the stockroom
recently incarcerated at the Billerica Jail
will once again become constructive
citizens after appropriate rehabilitation.

about the author

Michael Casey was born in Lowell, Massachusetts and worked as a kettleman in a textile mill dye house in nearby Lawrence. His writing has appeared in America, Ararat; College English, The Los Angeles Times, New York Times, Rolling Stone and Student Lawyer. He is the author of Obscenities, Yale University Press, 1972.

SOME ADASTRA PRESS
BOOKS
&
CHAPBOOKS

Zoë Anglesey, *SOMETHNG MORE THAN FORCE: POEMS FOR GUATEMALA*, offset, perfect bound, 2nd printing, 1984

Michael Casey, *MILLRAT*, offset, sewn, expanded edition, 1999

Alan Catlin, *SHELLEY AND THE ROMANTICS*, letterpress, sewn, 1993

Jane Candia Coleman, *DEEP IN HIS HEART J.R. IS LAUGHING AT US*, letterpress, sewn, 2nd printing, 1991

Jim Daniels, *NIAGARA FALLS*, offset, perfect bound, 2nd printing, 1995

W.D. Ehrhart, *BEAUTIFUL WRECKAGE: New & Selected Poems*, offset, perfect bound, 1999

W.D. Ehrhart, *THE OUTER BANKS & Other Poems*, offset, perfect bound, 4th printing, 1984

W.D. Ehrhart, *THE DISTANCE WE TRAVEL*, offset, perfect bound, 2nd printing, 1994

Geoffrey Jacques, *SUSPENDED KNOWL-EDGE*, letterpress, sewn, 1998

Linda Lee Harper, *BLUE FLUTE,* letterpress, sewn, 1999

Richard Jones, *SONNETS*, letterpress, sewn, 1990

Joseph Langland, *TWELVE POEMS with Preludes and Postludes*, offset, perfect bound, 3rd printing, 1989

Christopher Locke, *HOW TO BURN*, letterpress, sewn, 1995

Thomas Lux, *THE BLIND SWIMMER: Selected Early Poems, 1970-1975*, offset, perfect bound, 1996

Thomas Lux, *THE DROWNED RIVER*, offset, perfect bound, reprint, 1994

Gary Metras, *DESTINY'S CALENDAR* , offset, perfect bound, reprint, 1988

Gary Metras, *THE NIGHT WATCHES*, letterpress, sewn, 1981

Gary Metras, *SEAGULL BEACH*, letterpress, sewn, 1995

Stephen Philbrick, *UP TO THE ELBOW*, letterpress, sewn, 1997

David Raffeld, *INTO THE WORLD OF
MEN*, letterpress, sewn, 1997
Becky Rodia, ANOTHER FIRE, letter-
press, sewn, 1997
Miriam Sagan, POCAHONTAS DISCOV-
ERS AMERICA, letterpress, sewn,
1993
Tom Sexton, LEAVING FOR A YEAR, let-
terpress, sewn, 1998

§

Copies may be obtained from the pub-
lisher, through your Bookstore, or from

Small Press Distribution, Inc.
1341 Seventh Street
Berkeley, CA 94702
(1-800-869-7553)